WALL STREET
TALK

Wall Street Talk

How to Understand Your Broker

Barbara Gilder Quint
illustrated by Marjorie Lewis

WALKER AND COMPANY ❊ **NEW YORK**

First published in the United States of America in 1983 by the Walker Publishing Company, Inc.

Published simultaneously in Canada by John Wiley & Sons, Canada, Limited, Rexdale, Ontario.

ISBN: 0-8027-7232-3 (paperback)
          0-8027-0754-8 (hardcover)

Library of Congress Catalog Card Number: 83-40042

Printed in the United States of America

10 9 8 7 6 5 4 3 2 1

To George

Introduction

Traditionally, economics has been known as the "dismal science," and financial professionals have been shrugged off as practitioners of a dull trade. In truth, however, managing money can be a sprightly business, and the language of finance often reflects this spirit. Who, for example, could possibly be bored by a discussion of a takeover attempt featuring "killer bees," "cyanide capsules," and "sex without marriage?" Or an analysis of portfolio theory that includes such words as "closet indexers" and "naked options"? These and similar terms are rapidly entering the business jargon and are making it increasingly difficult to discuss investments with your money manager or broker.

To save sophisticated investors the embarrassment of not understanding this new, esoteric language, I felt it was time to prepare an up-to-date guide listing the more frequent and colorful terms. I hope you will enjoy adding these words to your vocabulary, using them coolly and stylishly with your broker, your trust officer, or your next dinner partner. Picture the look on his face as you coyly ask him if he's a "closet indexer"!

Barbara Gilder Quint

ADRs

Abbreviation for American Depository Receipts: securities representing shares in a foreign company, issued by a United States bank. An investor seeking to purchase shares in such foreign companies as Hitachi or De Beers would find it much easier to buy and sell ADRs than to deal in the actual foreign shares. And since the ADRs represent the foreign shares, they will move up and down in price as do the actual shares.

AIR-POCKET STOCK

A stock that, following the announcement of bad news about the company, trades at a much lower price, perhaps 20 percent to 25 percent below the preceding sale price. For example, late in the afternoon of June 12, 1983, Texas Instruments disclosed that it expected a loss of as much as $100 million for its June quarter. The stock had closed at 157¾; the next morning it opened at 119, down 38¾.

That gap between 157¾ and 119 would be called an air pocket, and any stock vulnerable in this way to similar losses, perhaps because of a previous run-up and/or a high price-earnings multiple, is referred to as an air-pocket stock.

Annuity

A contract under which a person gives an insurance company a sum of money either in one payment (a single-payment annuity) or in yearly installments. In exchange, the company promises to pay the person a given amount at some future date. For example, in a typical annuity, a seventy-five-year-old woman might give an insurance company $10,000 in exchange for its promise to pay her $133.32 per month for the rest of her life, beginning at once.

Arbitrage

A way of making money by taking advantage of differences in the prices of equivalent items. For example, assume White Corp. is selling at $24 a share and Black Corp. at $50. Black makes an offer to exchange one share of Black for two shares of White. An arbitrageur might purchase two hundred shares of White for $4,800 (two hundred × $24), simultaneously selling one hundred shares of Black for $5,000. He plans to use the two hundred shares of White to produce the required one hundred shares of Black, and thus earn an arbitrage profit of $200 (less expenses) on the transaction.

Most arbitrageurs are financial professionals who specialize in this kind of operation, but individual investors occasionally make money in this fashion, too.

Backwardation

A term used to describe a situation in trading foreign exchange or commodities in which the farther in the future the delivery month, the lower the price. For example, if futures contracts to buy June gold are selling at $419, July contracts at $417, August contracts at $414, and so on, backwardation would be at work. (See also CONTANGO.)

Bang the Board

An expression that refers to aggressive buying or selling of money-market futures on the Chicago Board of Trade.

BANs, TANs, and TRANs

Various forms of short-term debt sold by states and other municipalities, usually coming due in a few months to a year from the time of issue. Bond Anticipation Notes (BANs) are sold in anticipation of the fact that the issuer plans to pay them off by selling a long-term bond issue in the near future; Tax Anticipation Notes (TANs) will be paid off from taxes to be collected in the near future, and TRANs (Tax and Revenue Anticipation Notes) will be redeemed, when due, from the proceeds of taxes and other expected revenues.

Basis points

A convenient way of expressing small differences in yields or interest rates. Each percentage point is divided into one hundred basis points. Thus a bond yielding 9.27 percent is said to be yielding six basis points more than a bond paying 9.21 percent; a Treasury bond yielding 9½ percent is said to be yielding fifty basis points less than a corporate bond yielding 10 percent.

Bearer Bond

A bond that does not carry the owner's name on it, merely stating that the principal is payable at maturity to the "bearer." The issuer of the bond does not have a record of the owner and therefore cannot send him his interest payments; instead, the owner collects interest by clipping coupons attached to the bond and depositing them in his bank.

Under new federal legislation, no bearer bonds will be issued after July 1, 1983. (The IRS has long claimed that the anonymity provided by these bonds makes it possible for many to evade income taxes and estate taxes.) Instead, all new bonds will come in registered form, where the owner's name appears on the face of the bond and is kept on record by the issuer; interest will be payable by check from the issuer. However, billions of dollars' worth of old bearer bonds issued in previous years will be around for decades. (See also REGISTERED BONDS.)

Bear Market

A market in which prices are falling, a "bear" being someone who anticipates lower prices. It is thought that the term *bear* came to be used to describe a declining market because bears pull down when fighting. Conversely, the term *bull* may be used to describe a rising market because bulls rear up.

Beta

A measure of how much a stock will move in comparison with the rest of the market. A stock with a beta of 1, such as IBM, will go up or down (percentagewise) at about the same rate as the Dow Jones or Standard & Poor's averages. A beta of less than 1 indicates that the stock is less volatile than the market (AT & T has a beta of .65), while a stock with a beta greater than 1 will swing more than the market (Federal Express's beta is 1.6). Example: An investor owns a portfolio heavily weighted with stocks rather than bonds. However, the average beta of his stocks is considerably under 1, so even if the market falls out of bed, his portfolio shouldn't be severely affected.

Check with your broker for a listing of the betas on stocks you hold, or look them up yourself in *The Value Line Investment Survey,* available at your local library.

Big Board

The New York Stock Exchange.

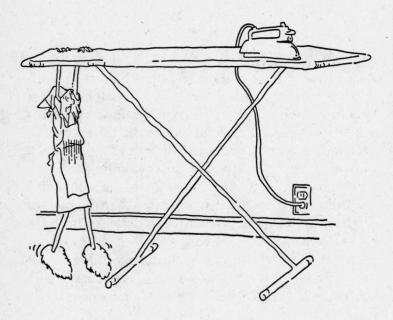

The big board

The big eight

Big Eight

The eight most prestigious major accounting firms: Price Waterhouse, Arthur Andersen & Co., Arthur Young & Co., Deloitte Haskins & Sells, Peat Marwick Mitchell & Co., Coopers & Lybrand, Touche Ross, and Ernst & Whinney. These firms are used by most of the largest U.S. corporations; hence, one sign that a small, regional corporation is thinking about achieving big-company status might be a move from using its old accountant to using one of the big-eight firms.

Big Figure

A term used to denote the first three numbers of the price in trading foreign currencies. For example, if the British pound is selling at $1.6213, the big figure would be $1.62.

The big figure

Blue Chip

A somewhat subjective term, intended to identify a company that the speaker feels is classy, with well-known products or services and a good financial record. The problem with this term is that evaluation of "classiness" varies from speaker to speaker, and that yesterday's blue chips (say, International Harvester or Johns Manville) may well turn out to be one of today's *cats and dogs*. (See also CATS AND DOGS.)

Blue List

A daily publication, printed on blue onionskin paper, listing municipal and corporate bonds offered for sale by bond dealers. The Blue List is available at brokers' offices and most banks; your broker might perhaps consult it if you wanted a quote on a particular municipal bond that you owned or if you wanted to see what bonds were available for possible purchase.

Blue-sky laws

Blue-sky Laws

Laws passed by states to protect investors. The term traces its origin to a remark by a Kansas legislator that unless his state passed effective legislation, promoters would try to sell shares of stock in the blue sky to unsuspecting investors.

Boiler Room

A sales organization using high-pressure methods to sell investments of dubious value. The term is based on the typical setup of many such operations: a room, often a basement in a low-rent district, equipped with many telephones. Each telephone is equipped with a smooth-talking salesperson armed with a list of potential suckers and a prerehearsed spiel. The noise from the salespeople and the general ambiance of the establishment make it similar to a boiler room.

Boneyard

Nickname for the Federal Reserve Bank of New York.

Bottom Trawler

An investment group that hopes to buy out a certain property or a subsidiary of a troubled corporation at a bargain price.

Boutique

A Wall Street term for a small brokerage firm that emphasizes one particular service—usually research—rather than providing the full range of services that the big firms do. Because of recent pressure on commission rates, most boutiques are in trouble, and many have merged with full-service firms. (See also MAY DAY.)

Breadth of the Market

A term referring to various measurements that indicate how most stocks have been acting—an alternative to relying on guidelines like the Dow Jones or Standard & Poors averages, which measure the performance of only a limited number of stocks. One widely used breadth-of-the-market indicator is how many individual stocks are up and how many are down on any given day. If the Dow Jones average is up, but most individual stocks are down, the market is said to be suffering from "bad breath."

Bucket shop

Buba

A nickname used by foreign-exchange traders for the Bundesbank, the West German Central bank.

Bucket Shop

A dishonest brokerage house. The term comes from one formerly used to describe a "low ginmill where beverages were dispensed in small amounts in buckets," and where, as a sideline, small speculations took place.

Bull Market

A market where prices are rising; thus, to be "bullish" is to expect higher prices.

Burying the Body

This expression refers to various methods used to conceal unhappy financial facts about a company by camouflaging them in a larger batch of numbers. For example, the consequences of the failure of a new product or a loss on a former investment might be buried under such obscure headings as "Miscellaneous" or "Other" in a quarterly or year-end earnings statement.

Butterfly Spread

In commodity trading, an arcane transaction involving three different contracts on a given commodity. For example, the client might buy one contract (say, September silver), sell another (March silver), and buy a third (December silver), in an attempt to take advantage of differences in price. Or, rather than using a buy-sell-buy butterfly, the client could work out a sell-buy-sell arangement. Butterfly spreads, in addition to being enormously complicated, also involve substantial commissions, which often eat up the profits—if there are any.

Burying the body

Butterfly spread

Cage

The part of the back office of a brokerage house or bank where the actual processing of securities takes place. The term comes from earlier days, when physical transfer of securities was more common, and when the securities—and the people who handled them—were protected in an area which could only be reached through a cagelike door or window.

Call

A call option on a stock works somewhat like an option on a piece of real estate; that is, it gives a client the right to buy that stock at a stated price during a stated period of time. For example, if he buys a call on 100 IBM at 125, good through March 25, he will have the right to insist that the person who sold him that call deliver to him one hundred shares of IBM at $125 each at any time through March 25.

Calls can be bought and sold through most brokerage firms. They trade on several exchanges, including the American Stock Exchange and the Chicago Board Options Exchange.

Callable Bonds

Bonds for which the issuer retains the right to redeem before the stated maturity or due date. The specific terms of a possible call are spelled out on the face of the bond, in its indenture, or in financial manuals published by Moody's and Standard & Poor (available at banks, libraries, and brokers, offices). These terms include the dates on which the bonds can be called and the price the holder will get if they are called (usually somewhat above $1,000).

Callable bonds can prove uncomfortable if the client buys them at a time when interest rates are high, figuring that he's locked in those high interest rates for a long period, because when interest rates decline, the company can call the bonds, leaving the client with money to reinvest in a period when available interest rates are much lower. One consolation, however, is that even those bonds that are callable usually offer some call protection; that is, they cannot be called for a stated period, often five to ten years, following their issue.

Noncallable bonds are those which the issuer cannot redeem before maturity. Among the most common of noncallable bonds are most of those issued by the U.S. Treasury. (See also INDENTURE.)

Cats and Dogs

Stocks in companies that are small, new, poorly financed, or in trouble. Note, however, that a fine way of making money on Wall Street is to seek out today's cats and dogs in the hope that they will turn into tomorrow's blue chips. Xerox, for example, was once an obscure company called Haloid and considered a cat-and-dog stock by many.

Chapter 11

The section of the Federal Bankruptcy Act which outlines one set of procedures that can be followed when a publicly-owned company goes bankrupt. The term has become a euphemism for saying that a company is in trouble; thus, if someone states that a particular company is "headed for Chapter 11," it means that the company is experiencing serious financial difficulties.

Chicago Pneumatic Tool Clause

This term refers to one of the first methods of discouraging unfriendly takeover bids; the clause requires approval of a merger from a supermajority—say 95%—of all the shares outstanding. This kind of measure was first introduced by the Chicago Pneumatic Tool Company in 1975. (See also SHARK REPELLENTS.)

Chips

The Clearing House Interbank Payments System. Run by the big commercial banks in New York through the New York Clearinghouse Association, this system is used to transfer money from one bank to another.

Chips

Clean Balance Sheet

A balance sheet with few, if any, debt or debt-like items, like leases. For example, a clean balance sheet might be one showing that the company has raised the long-term money needed for its operations primarily by selling common stock and retaining previous earnings, rather than borrowing money by selling bonds and preferred stock issues.

Clifford Trust

A legal arrangement whereby one may transfer income-producing assets, such as stocks or bonds, to a trust for the benefit of someone else—one's child, for instance. The income from the securites is taxed at the rate the child or trust would pay, a rate which is often much lower than one's own tax rate. The trust must remain in effect for at least ten years and one day, but at the end of the period, the original owner gets his property back.

Clifford trusts are an attractive arrangement for a parent who wants to shift income to a child's lower tax bracket during the parent's high-earning years, but who wants to get the property back eventually, perhaps because it will be needed after retirement. This is different from the more flexible Crown Loan because of the length of time one *must* leave the money in the trust.

Clifford trusts require expert legal help to set up, and there are many potential tax traps, which the attorney should review before proceeding. (See also CROWN LOAN.)

Closet Indexer

Indexing your investments involves choosing securities so that the resulting portfolio reflects one of the standard market averages. For example, if one were indexing in accordance with the Standard & Poor five hundred-stock average, and if 7 percent of the value of the stocks in that average consisted of IBM, then one would put 7 percent of one's money into IBM. Because of the enormous pressure on investment managers not to do worse than the averages, there is a temptation to use indexing as a way of insuring that the portfolios they manage perform at least as well as the averages. However, clients are not willing to pay managers a hefty fee merely for indexing since clients obviously could do so on their own. A closet indexer is one who manages money for clients, theoretically using his judgment to choose appropriate investments, but, in actuality, indexing the portfolio.

Closet indexer

Contango

Commercial Paper

A form of short-term borrowing used to raise money by high-grade companies and some municipalities. Investors often buy commercial paper—say, $25,000 of General Motors Acceptance Corp. commercial paper due in three months—as a safe, temporary "parking place" for money on which they can earn the going interest rate. Commercial paper can be bought from a bank or broker.

Contango

A term used to describe a situation in trading foreign currencies or commodites in which the further away the delivery month, the higher the price.
(See also BACKWARDATION.)

Contrary Opinion

The theory that whenever public investors become absolutely convinced the market will move in one direction, it will move in the other. (This concept reflects Bernard Baruch's dictum that the time to buy is when everybody else is selling and the time to sell is when everyone else was buying.) A person who adheres to this theory is called a "contrarian." (See also ODD LOT RATIO.)

Convertible Bonds

Bonds which, like the traditional bond, guarantee a stated amount of interest each year and repayment of the principal when the bonds come due. However, the issuer throws in an additional sweetener: at the investor's option, he may exchange each bond for a set number of shares of the company's stock. Thus, if he buys a $1,000 face value K-Mart Corp. 6 percent convertible bond of 1999, he'll get $60 a year in interest while he holds the bond, but if he wishes, he may exchange it at any time for 28.17 shares of K-Mart common stock. Should K-Mart prosper and the stock rise significantly—say, to $50 a share—the investor's bond would then be worth $50 X 28.17, or roughly $1,400.

Many financial experts feel that convertible bonds in good-quality companies offer the best of both worlds. If the stock declines in price, the investor sticks with the bond and collects his interest, but if the stock rises, he can participate in the rise because of the conversion feature. The exact terms of the conversion privilege—that is, how many shares the investor can get for each bond—varies with the bond and will be stated on the face of the bond, or can be obtained from a broker.

Cooking the Books

Any method of misrepresenting the true financial situation of a business through inaccurate or incomplete statements of actual numbers. For example, the treasurer of a given company might cook the books by reporting nonexistent inventories, managing to show the company as financially viable when, in truth, it is on the verge of bankruptcy.

Cooking the books

Counter Punching

This expression, used primarily in bond trading, describes trades made counter to (against) price movements. Thus, counter punching would involve buying when prices are going down or selling when prices are going up.

Coupon Rate

The interest rate stated on the face of a bond. For example, the coupon rate on the Nevada Power Co. 7$\frac{1}{8}$ percent bonds of 1998 is 7$\frac{1}{8}$ percent. (See also CURRENT YIELD, YIELD TO MATURITY.)

Cover

A term, used in connection with the Treasury's sales of new issues of U.S. Government debt, referring to the relationship between the total bids received for the issue and the actual amount offered. For example, a cover of 2 would mean that bids for twice the amount of the issue were submitted—say, $8 billion for an issue of $4 billion.

Counter punching

Covered Writer

The person who sells a call option is also known as the "writer" of the option. If the writer owns the underlying stock, then he is said to be "covered," or a "covered writer." For example, if John Smith sells a call on one hundred shares of General Motors at $60 each, he is in effect promising to deliver one hundred shares of GM on demand at $60 a share. If he owns the stock, he is known as a "covered writer." (See also NAKED OPTIONS.)

Crazy Eights

Bond traders' nickname for the 8 percent Treasury bonds due in 1986, a widely traded issue.

Crown Loan

A fairly new tax-cutting device named after Harry Crown, a Chicago industrialist who was one of the first to use it. Crown loans are interest-free demand loans, particularly useful as a way for parents to accumulate money to pay their children's college bills. Under such an arrangement, the parent lends the child money without charge and then invests this money, in the child's name, in high-paying bonds, stocks, or bank accounts. Because the money is in the child's name, income taxes are minimal, while if the money remained in the parent's name, the income would be taxed at a higher bracket. For example, if the parent lends his child $10,000 in a Crown Loan and invests the money in a bond paying 10 percent ($1,000) a year, then if this is the child's only income, there would be no tax at all on the interest paid, and the family could accumulate the entire $1,000 as part of a future college fund. On the other hand, if the $10,000 were in the parent's name and he were in the 40 percent tax bracket, he'd have to pay $400 of the $1,000 in income taxes, and the family would accumulate only $600 toward future college bills.

Crown loans may also be used where adult children are supporting elderly low-tax-bracket parents. Here, the parents borrow the money and invest it, shifting the income from the money into their lower tax brackets.

A lawyer should always be consulted for advice on establishing a Crown Loan and to review the most recent IRS rulings concerning the Crown Loan.

Crown loan

Current Yield

The actual rate of return you are currently receiving on monies invested in bonds. For example, if one buys a 6 percent bond with a face value of $1,000 but pays only $800 for it, each year one will earn $60 in interest on the bond. Since one paid only $800 for it, the current yield is $60, or 7½ percent. (See also YIELD TO MATURITY, COUPON RATE.)

Cyanide Capsule

"Taking a cyanide capsule" is one of the most drastic moves a company can make if threatened with an unfriendly takeover. The "cyanide capsule" is a big loan with a stipulation that the entire amount must be repaid immediately if the company is acquired. The object is to discourage a potential acquirer, who would be faced with the necessity of repaying an enormous sum at once if his takeover attempt were successful. (See also SHARK REPELLENTS.)

Debenture

A bond that is backed only by the general credit of the issuer, rather than by a specific asset. Generally speaking, only the higher-quality companies can sell debentures to investors; where there is more risk, investors will demand a specific asset as collateral. (See also MORTGAGE BONDS.)

Delayed Opening

A temporary hold on trading a particular stock. When there is an imbalance of buying and selling offers on the floor of a stock exchange—say, because of an unexpected bit of good news about a company issued late the preceding afternoon—a stock may not be traded for several hours or, in some extreme cases, even for several days, until the orders can be sorted out and a price established. Thus, if a client calls his broker at noon and asks where ABC Company opened following the previous day's announcement of a new oil discovery, the broker may tell him there's a delayed opening and that no trading of the stock has yet taken place.

Delayed opening

Discount Broker

A broker who buys and sells for his clients, charging commissions that are significantly lower than the standard rates currently being charged by the major brokerage firms. Discount-broker commissions can run one-third to one-half of the rates—say, $30 instead of $85 for selling one hundred shares of a $60 stock. Discount brokerage is generally offered on a limited-service basis; unlike accounts held at full-price brokerage houses, a client won't have access to research, advice, and hand holding from a broker. Instead, he'll deal with an order taker, who will merely execute orders to buy or sell securities.

Discount brokerage services are offered not only by brokerage houses, but also by a growing number of banks. Advertisements for discount brokers, often stating the commissions they charge, may be found on the financial pages in many leading newspapers.

Discount Rate

The interest rate that the Federal Reserve banks charge commerical banks for short-terms loans. This is a key interest rate, because it determines to a large extent the interest rates that commercial and other banks will charge their customers. Thus, if the Fed raises the discount rate, the odds are that interest rates throughout the economy will increase, too. The current rate is listed on the financial pages of leading newspapers.

Discretionary Account

An account in which the broker or someone else (the client's spouse, brother-in-law, or lawyer, for instance) has written permission to buy or sell securities at his discretion.

Disintermediation

The process through which individuals take their money out of savings accounts and invest directly in such alternative investments as Treasury bills or commercial paper, usually because these investments are paying higher interest than savings accounts. In financial jargon, the money is being withdrawn from the financial intermediaries—the banks—hence, the term *disintermediation*.

DJIA

An acronym for the Dow Jones Industrial Average, an average of the prices of thirty leading stocks on the New York Stock Exchange. Since the calculation of this average takes stock splits into account, it isn't an exact mathematical average of current prices. In addition, to reflect, the changing trends of American business, there are periodic changes in the stocks included in the average. For example, within the past few years, stocks of such heavy-industry companies as Kennecott have been replaced by high-technology companies, such as IBM, and service companies, such as American Express.

Two other similar averages are the Dow Jones Transportation Average—for stocks of airline, railroad, trucking, and similar companies—and the Dow Jones Utility Average.

DK

Abbreviation for Don't Know. Widely used by brokers when, in a busy market, a security is delivered to them from another broker, but they do not recognize the transaction because the price (or the number of shares, or even the name of the security) doesn't agree with their own records.

Don't fight the tape

Dollar Cost Averaging

A system for buying securities in which one invests an equal dollar amount each period—say, $1,000 every three months in Exxon stock. This method, by permitting a client to buy more shares of a stock when the price is down, has a built-in mechanism for taking advantage of temporary market sell-offs. For example, if the client is dollar-averaging Exxon, which is selling at $30 a share, $1,000 will buy roughly thirty-three shares; if it is selling at $25 a share, $1,000 will buy forty shares.

Don't Fight the Tape

Traditional Wall Street slogan meaning that if the stock market, or an individual stock, as reflected in transactions reported on the ticker tape, is going in one direction, an investor should take his cue from that trend—unless, of course, he's a contrarian! (See also CONTRARY OPINION.)

Dow Theory

A way of forecasting the state of the stock market based on the trends of the Dow Jones Industrial Average and the Dow Jones Transportation Average. According to this theory, the stock market is in a basic upward trend when one of these averages makes a new high that is then "confirmed" by a new high in the other average. Conversely, the market is said to be in a basic downward trend if the D-J Industrials sell off below their previous low, and then, soon afterward, the D-J Transportation Average also hits a new low.

Drain Week

A week in which the Federal Reserve apparently attempts to discourage bank lending and to raise interest rates by removing, or draining, sources of lendable money from the banks.

Equipment Trust Certificates

Certificates widely used by railroads to raise money for new equipment. For example, a railroad might sell equipment trust certificates to buy locomotives, with title to the locomotives held by a trustee (a bank, for instance) until the certificate holders have been paid off. If the railroad can't pay the interest or principal on its certificates, the holder of the certificate has first claim to possession of the locomotives.

Because of the backing provided by the equipment, these certificates are usually considered a high-grade, safe investment.

Fannie Mae, Ginnie Mae, and Sallie Mae

Three government-chartered agencies designated to buy up old loans from banks and similar lenders, who will then have the monies they receive from the agencies to make new loans. Ginnie Mae, for example, provides a bank with new lendable dollars by buying up its old FHA (Federal Housing Authority) or VA (Veterans Administration) mortgages; the bank will then use the dollars it gets from Ginnie Mae to provide new mortgage money to a batch of new home buyers. Ginnie Mae will then resell those old mortgages to other investors; including pension funds and individuals.

Fannie Mae is the nickname for the Federal National Mortgage Association (FNMA), Ginnie Mae for the Government National Mortgage Association (GNMA) and Sallie Mae for the Student Loan Mortgage Association (SLMA). All three agencies work in a similar manner—in each case their role is to provide new lending money to banks and similar lenders by buying up old loans currently on their books.

Fannie Mae, Sallie Mae, Ginnie Mae

Fed Time

The crucial half hour from 11:30 A.M. to noon, Eastern Standard Time, when the Federal Reserve banks are, according to tradition, most likely to buy and sell securities, thus affecting their prices.

Flat Tax

A proposed system which would require taxpayers to pay a uniform tax rate on all income above a stated amount—for example, 25 percent of all income over $15,000. A flat tax would replace the marginal tax system now in effect in the United States, whereby an individual's tax rate increases with his income. (For example, tax rates for a married couple in 1984 ranged from 11 percent on the taxable-income bracket $3,400–$5,500 to 50 percent on taxable income over $162,400.)

Flight to Quality

The decision to switch investments from lower-rated, riskier securities to higher-quality ones (for example, selling A-rated bonds to move into AAAs, or liquidating cats and dogs to switch to blue chips).

Floating-rate Bonds

Bonds whose interest rate, rather than remaining fixed, may be changed periodically by the issuer. The interest rate is tied to some widely-followed rate, such as the rate currently being paid on Treasury bills. An investor might buy a twenty-year floating-rate bond on which the interest rate would be changed every six months, always paying 2 percent more than the average rate on six-month Treasury bills during the preceding period.

If an investor owns a floating-rate bond and general interest rates rise, the increase will be reflected in interest rates on Treasury bills and therefore in the interest on his own bonds; if, on the other hand, he owned a traditional bond, with its fixed coupon-interest rate, he would continue to receive only the original, lower rate. (See also COUPON RATE.)

Flogging the Market

Trading very actively and in large amounts in foreign-currency markets.

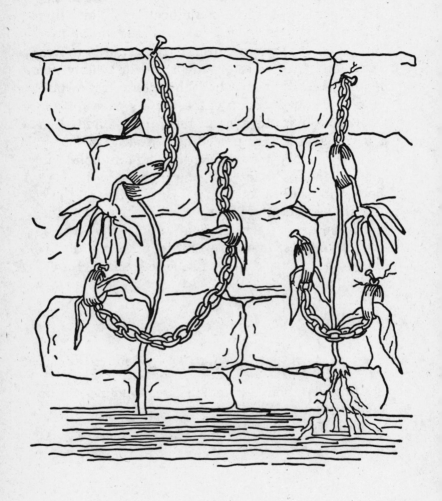

Flower bonds

Floor

A term often used to refer to the trading area where stocks and bonds are traded at the New York Stock Exchange. A floor broker is a member of the New York Stock Exchange who executes buy and sell orders on the floor of the Exchange. The term is also used in a similar manner when referring to the American Stock Exchange and other major exchanges.

Flower Bonds

Certain issues of U.S. Treasury bonds that can be applied at full face value to pay U.S. inheritance taxes. Since many of these bonds sell in the market for less than face value, they can be a sensible investment for someone who is about to leave an estate on which substantial taxes will be levied. Flower bonds include the 3½ percent Treasury bonds of February 1990, the 3 percent bonds of February 1995, and the 3½ percent bonds of November 1998.

Note that flower bonds can be used to pay estate taxes as long as they were purchased before death. Since, however, they pay much less in interest than other U.S. Treasury bonds, the best strategy is to wait as long as possible before buying them, rather than to accumulate them years ahead of time.

Fortune 500

Since 1958, Fortune magazine has published a list of the five hundred largest American industrial corporations, ranked according to size of sales. As a result of this list, it has become common Wall Street practice to identify one of these major corporations as a "Fortune 500 company." An analyst might indicate that a medium-sized company was growing rapidly by saying that although it wasn't a Fortune 500 corporation yet, it might be one shortly.

Freddie Mac

A close relative of Fannie Mae, Ginnie Mae, and Sallie Mae, Freddie Mac is the nickname for the Federal Home Loan Mortgage Corporation, which operates very much like those ladies. Specifically, Freddie Mac provides new mortgage money to such lenders as banks or mortgage companies by purchasing old, previously issued mortgages (different kinds from those dealt with by the ladies) from these institutions. (See also FANNIE MAE et al.)

Freddie Mac

Gilt-edged

A vague term used to describe a bond issued by a company which has earned so much in the past that there is no question about its ability to pay regular interest to its bondholders.

Going public

Going Public

When a company that is held primarily by insiders (the founding family, for instance) offers its stock for sale to outside investors for the first time, it is said to be "going public." (See also UNDERWRITERS.)

Gold Fix

A term used to designate the process by which London gold dealers establish the price of gold twice daily. Other world prices for gold are closely influenced by the gold-fix price.

Golden Parachute

A contractual arrangement designed to protect key executives of a company in the event of a takeover by an unfriendly outsider causing the executives to leave. Typically, a golden parachute might provide for a long-term employment contract, including extensive benefits, but permit the executive to cancel the contract after a takeover and leave the company while retaining his salary and benefits.

GOs

General Obligation bonds: municipal bonds backed by the full faith, credit, and taxing power of the municipality, as contrasted with revenue bonds, which are backed only by the revenues from a particular facility. For example, most turnpike bonds are revenue bonds; if the turnpike doesn't collect enough money from tolls and other fees to pay the investor his principal and interest, he has no further claim. On the other hand, most school-district bonds are GOs, since the district pledges, in effect, to raise real-estate and other taxes to whatever levels are necessary to meet interest and principal payments on its bonds.

GTC

Abbreviation for "good 'til canceled." The term refers to an order given to a broker to buy or sell securities that will remain in effect until canceled. Also called an "open order."

Haircutting the Overage

Technically speaking, deposits in banks and savings-and-loan associations are insured by the FDIC (Federal Deposit Insurance Corp.) and FSLIC (Federal Savings and Loan Insurance Corp.) up to only $100,000. However, in practice, in the past if a bank or savings-and-loan is liquidated due to financial difficulties, depositors are usually paid 100 percent of amounts even above that limit. "Haircutting the overage" would involve paying off only a percentage—say, 75 percent—of anything over the legally required $100,000. The objective would be to force big depositors to take a closer look at how safe their deposits would be in any given bank or savings-and-loan, thereby urging these institutions to adopt less risky business practices.

High Grades

A term used by bond dealers to designate general obligation municipal bonds rated AA or AAA. (See also GO.)

Hired Gun

An expert hired by a beleaguered company to fight off an unwelcome takeover. (See also KILLER BEES.)

Hit or Hitting the Bid

A hit occurs when an investor sells securities at the bid price quoted by the buyer. For example, if Exxon is quoted 34½–35, and if he wanted to sell, he would normally instruct his broker to try to get him a price somewhere in between. However, if he were nervous about the market, he might tell the broker to "hit the bid," settling for a sure $34½ per share, rather than hoping for more and possibly missing the market. In other words, if he absolutely, positively wanted to sell at no less than the current bid price, he would hit the bid.

HUD Note

A short-term debt issued by local housing agencies under the auspices of the Department of Housing and Urban Development. As such, these notes are backed not only by the local housing agencies, but also by the full faith and credit of the U.S. government. The notes are usually short-term—say, three months to a year—and the interest is tax-free since they have been issued by a local housing agency and therefore qualify as a municipal issue.

Because the notes are both tax-free and very safe, they are considered an ideal short-term parking place for money from nervous high-tax-bracket investors.

HUD notes are also known as "project notes" since the monies are used for temporary financing of housing projects.

Hypothecation

Generally used as an elegant term for what happens when an investor opens a margin account. It actually refers to the pledging of securities as collateral—precisely the procedure when one is "on margin."

Income Splitting

Various methods of switching income within a family so that some of it is reported on the tax returns of family members in lower tax brackets, rather than on the returns of family members in the higher brackets. (See also CLIFFORD TRUST, CROWN LOAN.)

Indenture

A written statement made when bonds are originally sold, setting forth all the terms of the bond issue. The terms include the amount and payment dates of the interest, the conditions under which the bonds may be redeemed or called before maturity, and any special obligations the issuer undertakes (such as maintaining certain balance-sheet standards). A broker can usually supply his client with a copy of the indenture for many bond issues; if not, the client should consult the trustee for the bond issue, whose name and address is given on the face of the bond itself.

Under normal circumstances, there would be no reason why anyone would want to look at the indenture for a bond issue—it's a deadly-dull booklet full of legal boilerplate. However, if the company issuing the bonds runs into trouble and defaults on its bonds, one might want to read it to see exactly what protection and rights the bondholder has.

In-the-money

A term used in trading call options to indicate an option where the strike price is below the market price. For example, if an investor buys a call on one hundred General Motors shares at $60 at a time when GM is selling at $62, then this would be an in-the-money call. With puts, the reverse applies, and an in-the-money put option would be one where the strike price was above the current market price. (See also STRIKE PRICE, PUT, CALL, OPTION.)

IRA Rollover

When an employee leaves a job—either at retirement or to take another position—he often receives a sum of money from his former company's pension or retirement or profit-sharing funds. Normally, these monies would be taxed. However, all immediate taxes can be avoided if, within sixty days of receipt, the money is "rolled over"—that is, placed with a new custodian, such as a bank or brokerage house. The new account is called an IRA rollover, and it can be invested, at the option of the owner, in a wide variety of investments including annuities, bank accounts, bonds, and stocks.

An IRA rollover account should not be confused with the regular IRA account to which one may now contribute a maximum of $2,000 to $2,250 a year. Both accounts involve a deferral of taxes until the money is withdrawn at some later date, but there is no limit on the lump-sum amounts that may be transferred from another retirement plan into an IRA rollover account; it may even run into the hundreds of thousands of dollars in the case of some highly-paid executives.

IRA rollover

Jumbo CD

A certificate of deposit issued by a bank or savings-and-loan association for an amount over $100,000 usually for a period of a year or less. Should not be confused with the time deposits of certificates of deposit, offered by banks and savings-and-loan associations for their retail customers and available for depositors in sums as small as a few hundred dollars. With these small CDs, there are special restrictions, such as penalties for early withdrawal, which may not apply to many of the jumbos.

Killer Bees

Law firms, proxy solicitors, and public-relations firms employed to help a company management fight off an unfriendly takeover. (See also SHARK REPELLENTS.)

Kiss Principle

Advice given by old pros to neophyte brokers on how they should explain to investors such sophisticated investment concepts as options and arbitrage. Stands for "Keep It Simple, Stupid."

Kiss principle

Krugerrands

Gold coins sold by South Africa, containing various standard amounts of gold—one-tenth, one-quarter, one-half, or one full ounce. They are considered a handy way of investing in gold as the price of the Krugerrand will fluctuate directly with the world price of gold. The most common Krugerrand is the one-ounce coin, which may be bought from coin dealers and some banks.

Laffer curve

An economic model widely used by the Reagan administration in the early 1980s to justify its tax policy. The curve indicates how much tax revenue the government will collect at different income-tax rates. For example, if the tax rate is zero, the government will collect nothing; if the tax rate is 10 percent, the government will collect a certain amount; if the tax rate is 15 percent, the government will collect more, and so forth. The curve also indicates, however, that after a certain point, when tax rates get too high, people will simply stop trying to earn more money because the government will take most of it, and that tax collections will therefore actually decline as income-tax rates increase.

The curve is named after Arthur B. Laffer, a California economist.

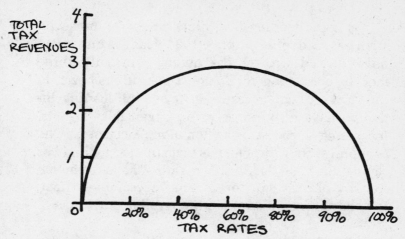

Theoretical Laffer curve. Note that nobody really knows where the curve peaks and at what tax rates it starts turning down.

Leading indicators

Certain economic factors whose trends "forecast" business conditions. For example, one leading indicator is the volume of new orders received by manufacturers of consumer goods, the production of which obviously increases or decreases accordingly. Another is the issue of building permits for private housing; since several months usually pass between the time a permit is granted and the start of construction, the number of permits issued should predict future housing activity. The index of leading indicators is compiled by the Department of Commerce each month, measuring twelve different factors.

Do the leading indicators work? In the seven business recoveries prior to 1983, leading indicators have turned up, on the average, roughly three months before general business conditions began to improve—a good record. However, the leading indictors have also, on occasion, given false signals, indicating a recession when none occurred. One economist, for example, has been quoted jokingly as saying that the leading indicators have been extremely effective in forecasting recession—in fact, they have forecast seven of the last five downturns.

Legal lists

Lists, prepared by individual states, of the securities in which certain institutions in the state—such as trust departments of banks—are allowed to invest monies for which they are fiduciaries or trustees. The lists vary from state to state, but the objective in each case is to reduce risk by limiting the names of the stocks and bonds on the list to high-quality securities.

LIFO

Acronym for Last In First Out, one way of determining how much the raw materials a manufacturer has taken from its inventory will actually cost when used in production. For example, assume a pot manufacturer holding two hundred pounds of copper in its inventory bought half of this copper two months ago at 75¢ a pound and the other half last month at $1.00 a pound. The manufacturer then withdrew one hundred pounds for current production purposes. Under LIFO accounting, $1.00 a pound would be the price set for the copper that goes into these new pots, and the profit reported on those pots would be based on a cost of $1.00 a pound for the copper.

Under FIFO accounting—First In First Out—the cost of the copper in those pots would be set at 75¢, giving the manufacturer a much larger profit to report after sales.

The terms LIFO and FIFO are often used by corporations in explaining sharp increases or decreases in their profit statements. For example, if the copper company described above had switched in the last year from FIFO to LIFO, and if during that year the price of copper had been rising, then the cost of the copper used in its production would be relatively high, and its profits would lower. In this case, the company report might state that profits were reduced because of a switch from FIFO to LIFO.

Limit order

An order placed with a broker to buy or sell securities at a specific price. For example, if an investor placed an order to sell 100 Ford at 62, he would be restricting or limiting his broker to selling the stock at $62 a share or above, but no less. (See also MARKET ORDER.)

Locked in

Uncomfortable position of an investor who has a substantial profit but feels he can't sell because of the sizable taxes that would be due on the profit. Sometimes the market solves the problem for the investor; that is, a severe decline in the price of the security occurs, wiping out both the profit and the potential tax liability.

Long-term investment

In a tax context, a long-term investment is one the investor has owned for more than a year and which therefore qualifies for long-term capital-gains treatment. This means that if he has a profit when he sells, only 40 percent of that profit is subject to federal income tax.

M-1 and M-2

These days financial analysts devote enormous attention to the "money supply"—the amount of money available for spending. The concept is that the more money is available, the more spending will occur, and vice versa. Under this assumption, government money managers like the Federal Reserve Board can control spending by controlling the supply of money. Thus, if there were too much spending in the economy and inflation threatened, the Fed might reduce the supply of money; if there were too little spending and growing unemployment threatened, the Fed could increase the supply of money.

One problem is how to measure the money supply. The original measurement was called M-1, which is primarily the amount of currency and checking account deposits. Another measurement is M-2, which adds a few other items to M-1, including the dollars in money market funds and savings accounts. In banking circles, M-1 is referred to as the "narrow" money supply, since it includes fewer items, while M-2 is often called the money supply "broadly defined."

Manny Hanny

Affectionate name for New York's Manufacturers Hanover Trust Company.

Margin call

A term generally referring to those unpleasant phone calls, wires, or letters from a broker asking his client to put up additional money or securities in an existing account. Such margin calls occur because the client bought securities on credit—say, putting up only half of the cost of the stock and borrowing the rest from his broker. Now the securities have dropped in price to the point where the broker is no longer willing (or legally permitted) to lend the client the outstanding amount, and he is therefore asking for additional assets to back up the loan.

Banks also send out margin calls on occasion, if the client has taken out a loan using stocks as collateral and these stocks decline in value to the point where the bank doesn't feel they are adequate collateral for the loan. (See also REGULATION T.)

Marital Deduction

A term used in estate planning to describe the amount of money that a married person may leave to a spouse free of federal estate taxes. Under 1981 revisions of the federal tax code, there is now an unlimited marital deduction; that is, a husband or wife may will to a spouse as much as he or she wishes without incurring any federal estate taxes whatsoever.

May Day

Market Order

An order placed to buy or sell securities at the most advantageous price currently available, without setting any specific price limit. (See also LIMIT ORDER.)

May Day

May 1, 1975. Prior to that date, all firms belonging to the New York Stock Exchange charged the same commission rates for their services. On that date, competitive commission rates were introduced under pressure from the SEC, and today, by shopping around, you can find N.Y. Stock Exchange brokerage houses whose rates are as little as one-half or even one-third of other firms' commissions. Wall Street old-timers divide their careers into a golden pre–May Day era, when commissions were fixed and high and business was often distributed on the basis of personal contacts, and the post–May Day era, one of fierce price competition.

MBIA-insured Bonds, AMBAC-insured Bonds

MBIA bonds are municipal bonds on which the payment of interest and principal is insured by a consortium of prominent insurance companies. The consortium is called the Municipal Bond Insurance

Association, and it includes Aetna Life & Casualty, St. Paul, and Travellers, among others.

A municipality that wishes to have MBIA insurance when it sells a new issue of bonds will take out a policy from MBIA, paying a one-time premium. From then on, any owner of the bonds has double-barreled protection; he has not only a guarantee of payments from the issuer itself but a guarantee from the insurance company consortium as well. Bonds insured by MBIA are automatically rated AAA, or highest-quality, by Standard & Poor, regardless of the rating that the municipality would have on its own.

AMBAC-insured bonds are very similar, but the insurance here is provided by the American Municipal Bond Assurance Corporation, a subsidiary of the MGIC Investment Corporation. Bonds with AMBAC insurance are also rated AAA by Standard & Poor.

MEGO

Acronym for Mine Eyes Glaze Over, an expression used to describe boring material. For example, typical mego reading might be the traditional prospectus or the footnotes at the back of a typical annual report. (See also PROSPECTUS.)

MIG-1, MIG-2, MIG-3

Three categories used by Moody's, an investment rating service, to rate the safety of short-term securities (usually one year or less) sold by states and other municipalities. MIG-1 is the highest rating. (The letters MIG stand for Moody's Investment Grade.) These categories are comparable to the AAA, AA, A, BBB, etc. ratings used by Moody to rate longer-term bonds. (See also BANs, TANs, and TRANs.)

Mortgage Bonds

A bond backed by a claim on a specific piece of property, such as a particular section of a railroad, an individual plant, or piece of equipment. In case of default, the bondholder has a prior claim to that property, a claim that comes before that of many of the other creditors. (See also DEBENTURE.)

Motorcycles

Bond-trader jargon referring to securities issued by the Federal Home Loan Mortgage Corporation and backed by the interest and principal payments to be received from a pool of mortgages held by the FHLMC.

Naked Option

Calls sold by a speculator on stocks he does not own.

Investors sometimes sell call options against stocks they own. Such options give the buyer the right to "call" or purchase the stock at a stated price during a stated period. For example, an investor might sell a six-month call on one hundred shares of General Motors at $70 a share, and this call would give the buyer the right to insist that the investor deliver to him 100 GM at 70 at any time during the six months. He would pay the investor a given amount—often several hundred dollars—for this call option.

If General Motors rises above $70 a share, the odds are that the buyer will request delivery of the stock; if the investor owns it, he may be unhappy at the thought of selling it at $70 rather than at the current higher price, but at least he *does* own the stock and can deliver it.

Some speculators, however, sell naked options. They assume that the stocks will not rise above the call price and that therefore they won't be asked for delivery. To continue with the above example, if GM falls to $65 a share, no one will exercise an option to buy it at $70. Obviously, however, the investor is headed for trouble if the stock does rise above the call price and he is "naked"—that is, he doesn't own it. In that case, he has various alternatives—including the extremely unpleasant one of going out and buying the GM stock in the open market at the higher price.

Naked option

NASDAQ

Acronym for the National Association of Securities Dealers Automated Quotations, an organization that does exactly what its name suggests. It provides a computerized information network through which brokers, banks, and other investment professionals can obtain up-to-the-minute price quotations on securities traded over-the-counter. The daily listing of prices for over-the-counter stocks which is found in many newspapers is provided by NASDAQ.

Years ago, before NASDAQ was in operation, brokers had to check the prices of over-the-counter stocks by telephoning three or four different dealers; now, they simply push a few buttons and the latest prices appear on a TV-like screen. (See also OVER THE COUNTER.)

Nifty Fifty

Another name for that batch of well-known high-growth stocks favored by many investment managers during the 1960s and 1970s, including Walt Disney, Eastman Kodak, IBM, Sears, and Xerox. Many of these stocks suffered sharp declines during the late 1970s, dropping to about a quarter of their former prices; some recovered most or all of these losses during subsequent years. A few, such as IBM, went on to sell at even higher prices, but an uncomfortable number were still, in mid-1983, selling substantially below their prices ten years earlier. (See also VESTAL VIRGINS.)

Nurd

No-load Fund.

A mutual fund that is sold to investors at the actual value of the underlying securities without an additional markup or commission. Load funds, on the other hand, are those for which the buyer pays the underlying value plus a load or commission of as much as 8½ percent.

NURD

Acronym for Negotiable Receipt of Deposit, also NRD.

NYFE (like "knife")

Acronym for the New York Futures Exchange, a subsidiary of the New York Stock Exchange where contracts in financial futures are traded.

NYSE Composite Index

An adjusted average of the prices of all stocks listed on the New York Stock Exchange. It is compiled several times a day and, along with the Dow Jones Industrial Average and the Standard & Poor 500, is widely used as a guide to the activity of the stock market.

Odd Lot

Anything less than the standard unit of trading. For example, on the New York Stock Exchange, where the typical round lot in most stocks is one hundred shares, an order to buy or sell anything between one and ninety-nine shares would be an odd-lot order. (See also ROUND LOT.)

Odd-lot Ratio

The ratio between how much stock the odd-lot customers are buying and how much they are selling. This figure is used as a measure of what the public is doing in the stock market. Every day, most major newspapers report the numbers of odd-lot shares purchased and sold on the New York Stock Exchange. For example, if two hundred thousand odd-lot purchases and one hundred thousand odd-lot shares are reported, the odd-lot ratio is two to one. Stock-market forecasters who are contrarians would view this as an indication that the small or public investors believe the market is headed higher (because they are buying more than they are selling) and that therefore the market will decline. Conversely, a sharp pickup in odd-lot selling would indicate that the public was bearish, and would be an indication to contrarians that the market was probably on an up trend. (See also BEAR MARKET, CONTRARY OPINION, ODD LOT.)

Outside director

Old Lady or Old Lady of Threadneedle Street

The Bank of England.

Option

A stock option is a contract permitting the holder to buy or sell one hundred shares of the designated stock at a specified price within a specified period of time. The two most common kinds of options are Puts and Calls. (See also PUT and CALL.)

Outside Director

The director of a corporation whose regular job does not include working for the corporation. Inside directors—the president or treasurer, for instance—are those who *do* work for the corporation. There is a general feeling today that the rights of the stockholders are best protected in a company where at least some of the directors are outside directors; in fact, at most major corporations, most of the directors *are* outsiders.

Over the counter

Pac-Man strategy

Over the Counter

Over-the-counter stocks and bonds are those which are not listed on an exchange, such as the New York Stock Exchange or the American Stock Exchange, where price information is obtained and orders executed right on the floor. Instead, over-the-counter securities are quoted through the NASDAQ information network, and orders are executed by phoning or telexing the brokers or dealers whose prices are shown on NASDAQ. Many stocks and almost all bonds are traded in the over-the-counter market, rather than on one of the exchanges. (See also NAS-DAQ.)

Pac-Man Strategy

A company strategy used to fight unfriendly takeovers. Involves making a tender offer for the stock of the company which is trying to take over. For example, when Martin Marietta was confronted by a hostile takeover bid from Bendix, one move it took to defend itself was to make a counter offer for the stock of Bendix itself. (See also SHARK REPELLENT.)

Painting the Tape

An illegal maneuver used by market manipulators to attract suckers. Here, the manipulator enters orders to buy a substantial amount of a stock at ever-increasing prices. As the stock is purchased, reports of the trade appear on the ticker tape, creating the impression that there is great activity in that company and hence good reason to invest in the stock. At this point in an effective painting-the-tape scheme, outsiders who are watching the tape will decide to buy the stock, and, as their buying pushes the stock higher, the manipulators will unload their own holdings

Paper Profit, Paper Loss

An unrealized profit or loss that exists only on paper because the investor hasn't finalized the transaction by actually selling the security. For example, if an investor bought one hundred shares of Gulf Oil at $25 a share and it is now selling at $35, he has a paper profit of ten points on one hundred shares, or $1,000, but it won't become an actual profit until he sells the stock.

Pareto's Law

In the early 1900s, an Italian economist, Vilfredo Pareto, observed that events are not equally distributed throughout the population and that a small percentage of events (20 percent) usually yields the majority of results (80 percent). The same rule applies to your investments: 80 percent of your profits will come from 20 percent of your stocks. The problem is knowing in advance which 20 percent.

Penny Stocks

Generic term for very low-priced stocks—sometimes selling at a few pennies a share, sometimes for a dollar or two—in very speculative companies. The Denver Stock Exchange and various Canadian stock exchanges have traditionally specialized in trading these stocks; the New York Stock Exchange and the other classier exchanges won't list them.

Pink Sheets

Listings of over-the-counter stocks, the dealers who trade them, and the prices at which these dealers are willing to buy and sell. Printed daily on loud pink newsprint and found in most brokerage houses and many banks.

Pip

The last digit in a five-figure foreign-currency quote. For example, if the price of the British pound is quoted at $1.6213, the pip would be 3. (See also BIG FIGURE.)

Premium

If an investor buys a bond for a price above its eventual value at maturity (which is $1,000), he has paid a premium for it. If he buys a bond for $1,040, he is paying a $40 premium. Note, however, that in many situations, paying a premium makes sense— for example, if the interest rate on the premium-priced bond is higher than that available on other comparable bonds priced at $1,000.

A bond bought for less than $1,000 is, in bond jargon, bought at a discount. Thus, a bond selling at $940 is priced at a discount of $60.

Price Earnings Ratio, or P/E

The relationship between the amount of money a company is earning on each share of stock and the price of the stock. For example, assume the Gee Whiz Co. is earning $2 million this year and has one million shares outstanding, so that it is earning $2 per share. If the stock is selling at $16 a share, then the ratio between the price ($16) and the earnings per share ($2) is 8; in other words, the stock is selling at a price/earnings ratio of 8. All other things being equal, the lower the P/E ratio, the more attractive the stock should be.

As of July 1, 1983, the average price/earnings ratio for a representative group of stocks (those in the Standard & Poor 500 stock average) was about 11. P/Es are listed along with stock quotations in most financial publications.

Prime Rate

The interest rate on loans which a bank is charging its best, most credit-worthy business customers. This interest rate affects all borrowers—not merely those who actually pay the prime—because the level of the prime rate and the direction in which it is moving tend to determine other interest rates. If the prime rate has been declining, it is likely that the rate other business borrowers pay—along with the rates consumers pay on mortgage, automobile loans, and personal loans—will soon be headed lower, too.

The prime rate is reported every day in the *Wall Street Journal* and on the financial pages of many other newspapers.

Prime rate

Prospectus

A booklet provided to prospective investors when certain securities, like new issues, are offered initially. The Securities and Exchange Commission regulations require that considerable information be given to these prospective buyers. A prospectus, which may run anywhere from a few pages to several hundred, will generally include extensive data on the company's business, assets, earnings and management, and will also give specific provisions of the securities themselves—for example, if they are bonds, it will review any call provisions. Prospectuses are notoriously dull and unreadable; although they are intended by law to inform investors, they usually succeed only in boring them.

Prudent-Man Rule

First spelled out back in 1830 by a Massachusetts jurist, Samuel Putnam, the rule defines certain acceptable investments as those that men of "prudence, discretion, and intelligence" would buy for themselves "in regard to the permanent disposition of their funds, considering the probable income as well as the probable safety of their capital." It is now used by many banks, trust officers, and pension-fund managers to justify investment decisions. For example, it is prudent to lose a client's money in IBM or Xerox; it is imprudent to lose it in iced-broiler futures or Australian uranium stocks.

Put

An option giving the person who owns it the right to sell one hundred shares of stock at a given price during a given period. For example, the nervous owner of one hundred shares of Eastman Kodak, currently selling at $81 a share, might buy a 3-month put on 100 Eastman Kodak at 80. This would give him the right to sell 100 EK at 80 at any time until the expiration date of that put; as a result, he could sleep soundly even if the price of the stock fell sharply.

Puts are complicated investment vehicles; one should check them out carefully with a broker before plunging ahead. If you want more help in understanding the options market, I suggest a book called *The New Options Market* by Max Ansbacher, also published by Walker and Company.

Q-Tip Trust

A Qualified Terminable Interest Property Trust, which permits a married person to leave all or part of his or her estate in trust, with the income from the trust to go to the spouse during that spouse's lifetime, but naming the person to whom everything will go after the spouse dies.

Q-TIP trusts are often useful in the case of a second marriage where, for instance, a wife wants to provide for her new husband during his lifetime but also wants to be sure that her property goes to her children after his death.

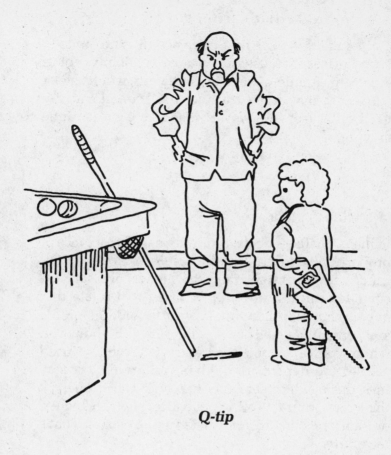

Q-tip

Radar Alert

Close watch by a company's top executives on trading in the company's stock. The objective is to turn up any unusual amount of buying which might indicate that someone is attempting to acquire a chunk of the stock in anticipation of a takeover attempt.

Random-Walk Theory

Claims that a stock's past price action is no guide to future prices, because prices move randomly, not in a pattern. Random-walk theoreticians would sneer at the idea that because a stock has been moving up during the last few weeks, it is likely to continue moving up.

Recapture

In many business deals, profits taken when a piece of property is sold are taxed at the favorable capital-gains tax rates rather than the higher, ordinary income-tax rates. For example, when real estate that one has held for more than a year is sold, the profits are generally taxed as capital gains. If, however, while you've owned the real estate, you've used accelerated depreciation (giving additional tax savings during the years one has held the property), then one would probably have to pay the higher, ordinary income-tax rates when a sale occurs. That's recapture.

Random-walk theory

Red Herring

The preliminary prospectus. This twenty to two-hundred-page-long booklet is given to a prospective purchaser of a new issue of securities during an interim period after certain forms have been filed with the SEC but before full information about the issue (e.g., price) is available. Contains incredible amounts of detailed information, much of it in jargon and therefore unreadable. You can tell it from the final prospectus by the hedge clause printed in bright red (hence the term *red herring*) on the front cover. (See also PROSPECTUS.)

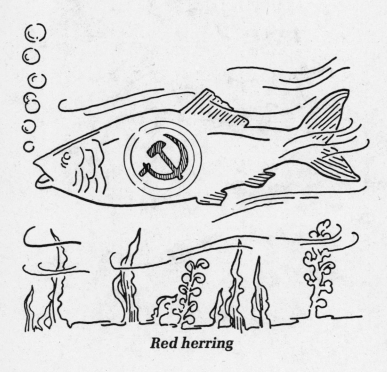

Red herring

Registered Bonds

A bond for which the name of the owner is listed on the face of the bond and on the books of the issuer. The owner gets interest in the form of checks sent to him directly by the company or its agent. Today, almost all newly issued bonds are available only in registered form. (See also BEARER BONDS.)

Registered Rep

Stockbrokers who are "registered" with the New York Stock Exchange or with the National Association of Securities Dealers, after having met certain personal and business standards and passed an exam. Also known as an "account executive" or "customer's broker."

Regulation T/Regulation U

Two Federal Board regulations controlling, respectively, the amount of credit a broker or bank can extend to a client to buy securities. During recent years, under Regulation T (applying to brokers), the Fed has set margin requirements on most stocks at 50 percent, meaning that the broker can lend a client no more than 50 percent of the cost of stocks he wishes to purchase. Regulation U applies in a similar manner to banks.

Repo or Repurchase Agreement

A sale of a security by a dealer with the understanding that he will buy it back at a particular price at some specified future date. Used primarily by big traders in the bond market, particularly with Treasury issues. (Do not confuse REPOs with the retail repurchase agreements or repos offered to savers by local banks and savings-and-loan associations as an alternative to the conventional savings accounts.)

Resistance Level

If a stock is trading at a price somewhat below the price at which a good deal of buying and selling took place previously, the old level is said to represent "resistance." For example, if General Motors traded between $65 and $68 per share for three months late last year, and then declined to $60, the 65–68 price range would be considered a resistance level. The theory is that all the investors who bought it last year at 65–68 and then saw it decline will want to get out once they are even. Moreover, they will be joined in selling by other, longer-term investors who are also unhappy because they didn't take advantage of the previous move to 65–68 to unload their GM stock. As a result, there will be considerable selling once the stock hits the 65–68 level again, and GM will "resist" moving above that level. (See also SUPPORT LEVEL.)

Round Lot

A standard unit of trading—for example, in a grocery store, the round lot in eggs is a dozen. On the New York Stock Exchange, the typical round lot is one hundred shares; in bonds, it is generally $1,000 or $5,000 face value. (See also ODD LOT.)

Safe Harbor

Another way of fighting off an unfriendly takeover by another company. Here, the company that is the object of the takeover goes out and buys a radio station, airline, or similar business, under the assumption that ownership of a subsidiary in such a heavily regulated industry will make acquisition of the company less attractive. (See also SHARK REPELLENTS.)

Saturday-Night Special

An unexpected takeover bid, usually by an unfriendly company whose object is to buy enough stock to achieve control before the present management of the company can rally support for itself.

Scale Order

An order to a broker to buy or sell amounts of a security at specified price variations. For example, if an investor owned eight hundred shares of Chrysler, he might instruct his broker to sell one hundred shares at $25¼, one hundred at 25½, and so on, with one hundred shares to be sold each time the stock rose one-quarter of a point. In this way, he'd hope to take advantage of a further move in the price of the stock. Similarly, if he wanted to buy five hundred shares of Deere & Co., he might enter a scale order to buy one hundred shares at $35 each and then one hundred additional shares every time the stock dropped a half point.

Seat

Common expression for a membership on an exchange. Thus, if someone "buys a seat" on the New York Stock Exchange, he becomes a member of the Exchange and can buy and sell securities there. As of July 1, 1983, the most recent sale of a seat on the New York Stock Exchange took place at $400,000.

Scale order

Selling Short

A maneuver in which an investor sells securities he does not own in the hope of buying them back later at a lower price. For example, if an investor thought that Mobil, currently selling at $40 a share, would soon report lower earnings and subsequently decline to $35, he might instruct his broker to sell one hundred shares short at $40. His game plan would be to deliver the stock he had just sold by buying one hundred shares at $35 after the bad news came out and the stock dropped.

Serial Bond

One of an issue of bonds in which some mature each year, rather than all at the same time. For example, a school district might sell a $2,000,000 issue of serial bonds, with $200,000 coming due each year over the next ten years.

Sex Without Marriage

An expression used to describe the final outcome when extensive negotiations between two companies planning to merge lead to greater familiarity, but no merger.

Serial bond

Sex without marriage

Shallow River Running Fast

A Wall Street term referring to significant change in the price of securities as a response to unsubstantiated rumors.

Shark Repellents

Various methods of protecting an entrenched management from outsiders who might want to take over the company. Typical shark repellents include amendments to the corporate charter requiring "supermajorities"—say, 90 percent or more of the shareholders—to approve certain kinds of takeover; staggered boards, where only part of the board of directors is elected each year; and fair-price proposals, where anyone buying some of the stock in order to obtain control must pay at least an equal price for the rest. (See also KILLER BEES, SAFE HARBOR, STAGGERED BOARDS.)

Shark repellent

Shelf Registration

Here a corporation wishing to sell new stocks or bonds to the public can file a single plan with the Securities and Exchange Commission, outlining its intentions to sell such securities over the next two years. Once the plan—called a registration statement—has been filed and is sitting "on the shelf" at the SEC, the corporation may then sell all or part of the securities, without any further procedures, at any time it feels market conditions are right.

Prior to the introduction of shelf registration in March 1982, a company usually had to file a new registration statement each time it planned to sell securities, a time-consuming procedure that could delay a sale by weeks or months, by which point the market might no longer be favorable for such a sale.

SIPC (pronounced "Si-pick")

Acronym for the Securities Investor Protection Corporation, a corporation created by Congress (although not a government agency) which will provide funds to protect investors' cash and stocks left with brokers who are covered by SIPC should the brokerage firm fail. There are, however, definite limits to the amounts SIPC will provide and to the circumstances under which such payments will be made; in addition, SIPC payments to investors can be very slow in coming.

Investors often tend to equate SIPC protection of their brokerage accounts with FDIC or FSLIC protection of their bank accounts, but the protection offered by SIPC is in fact much less extensive in many cases.

Six-Packs

Any money-market instrument (such as a certificate of deposit) issued by the Security Pacific Bank.

Six-packs

Sleeping Beauty

A desirable company, often with considerable cash on its balance sheet, that is vulnerable to a takeover attempt by another company.

Sleeping beauty

Snugging Up

A new term, first used in late 1982, which describes subtle, barely discernable steps taken by the Federal Reserve Board to nudge interest rates higher by reducing the lending capacity available to banks. For example, a *New York Times* financial reporter quoted a securities dealer as saying, sometime in mid-1983, "There are those who think the Fed has snugged a notch, those who think they have snugged two notches, and those who think they have not snugged at all."

Specialist

A member of the New York Stock Exchange who handles much of the trading in a particular stock. For example, if Ford is selling at $50 a share, and an investor places an order to sell it at 51, the floor broker for his brokerage house cannot wait around the Ford trading post indefinitely in the hope that Ford will reach 51. Instead, he gives the client's order to the specialist in Ford, who remains at the Ford trading post permanently, and who will try to execute the order when the price of the stock reaches the specified limit. The specialist will receive a small part of the commission the client pays his broker as his fee for handling the order.

A specialist is also responsible for maintaining an "orderly market" in "his" stocks. This means that he is committed to buying and selling his stocks for his own account if there is a temporary gap between buy orders and sell orders from outside customers. For example, if a sudden flood of buy orders for Ford reaches the floor of the New York Stock Exchange when the stock is selling at 52, the specialist might be required to sell stock from his own account so that the stock moves up only a point or two, in gradual steps, rather than suddenly jumping four or five points.

Spread

A term used on Wall Street in many different ways. One common usage refers to the difference between the bid and the asked price of a stock. For example, if Ford is quoted 50¼ bid but offered at 50½, the spread is one-quarter of a point. On widely traded securities, the spread tends to be small; on stocks or bonds that trade infrequently, spreads are larger; on some municipal bonds, the spread may be four points, or $40 to $50 per $1,000 bond.

Staggered Board

A board of directors in which only a certain number of the directors—say, a third—are elected each year. This is considered one effective method through which a company might protect itself against an unwelcome takeover attempt. With a staggered board, an outside group could only obtain control of a minority of the board of directors in any given year, since holdover directors elected in earlier years would continue to serve. (See also SHARK REPELLENTS.)

Standard & Poor's or S & P

Standard & Poor's Corporation is a financial-services firm well known for a variety of services and products. It compiles the Standard & Poor 500-stock index, an index of the prices of 500 leading stocks, which many people use as a guide to the general activity of the stock market. It also rates bonds, ranging from AAA for the safest, best-quality bonds, down to D for those in default. In addition, it publishes a large amount of statistical information about securities. Therefore, a good source for any information on the terms of a stock or bond issue, the earnings of the company, the prices of stocks or bonds in the past, would be one of the S & P services available at most libraries or brokers.

Stock Ahead

A phrase used by floor brokers to describe a situation where there are other orders at a client's price on the books of the specialist which must be executed before the client's since they were received earlier. For example, if a client enters an order to sell one hundred Penney at 60½, he may watch the tape and see Penney trade at 60½, but when his broker checks, the floor broker reports that the 60½ sale was not his, because there was "stock ahead." (See also SPECIALIST.)

Stock Split

The division of the shares of a corporation into a larger number of shares, each shareholder receiving his proportionate amount. For example, in 1979, IBM split 4 for 1, increasing the number of shares outstanding fourfold, from roughly 140 million to 560 million. As a consequence, a shareholder who formerly owned 50 shares of the "old," presplit stock suddenly owned 200 shares instead.

Splits must be proposed by the directors of a company and approved by the shareholders. All other things being equal, a split will be reflected more or less in the price of the stock, at least for the time being. Thus, right before the 1979 four-for-one split, IBM was selling around $300 a share; following the split, it sold around 75.

Stock splits are usually proposed by the directors of a corporation because they believe that the price of the stock has reached a level which discourages potential investors. Investors tend to prefer buying shares in increments of one hundred, and if a stock is selling at a high price—say, $120—they won't be able to afford one hundred shares. By splitting the stock, directors provide for a lower market price, which, theoretically, should attract investors.

Stock Symbols: GRRR, etc.

All stocks that are listed on exchanges, and many over-the-counter stocks, have symbols. Usually of two, three or four letters, they are used to identify the stock price information in the computer and to report trades. Most stock symbols are fairly routine. IBM for International Business Machines, XON for Exxon, GF for General Foods. Every once in a while, however, the people who assign them come up with an inspired choice. Almost everyone's favorite is the symbol for Lion Country Safari, the company that runs an amusement park and wild animal farm: it's GRRR. Other delightful symbols include NUTS, for Nutrition World; DOC, for Dr. Pepper; ACES for American Casino Enterprises and KIDS for The Children's Place.

Grrr

Stop-Loss Order

An order placed at a price below the market—for example, an order to sell 100 Woolworth at 20½ which is entered when Woolworth is selling at 22. Should Woolworth decline to 20½, the stop-loss order becomes a market order and the stock is then sold at the best price available. (This price may by 20½, or more or less than 20½. It is important for anyone who enters a stop-loss order to know that the order doesn't guarantee a sale at the specific price; it merely insures that the stock will be sold at the best price available at that time.) Stop-loss orders are used to protect gains or limit losses, guaranteeing the investor that if the stock declines to a predetermined point, it will automatically be sold, so he won't have to take the risk of staying with it if it moves down even more.

Street

Short for Wall Street, and also used to refer to the brokerage community in general, as in "street name." (See also STREET NAME.)

Street Name

Many investors leave their securities at their broker-age firms in the name of their broker, rather than having the securities registered in their own names. This is done either for convenience—for example, if the investors buys and sells frequently, or it may be required by the broker if the customer has a margin account and has borrowed part of the cost of the stock and the broker wants to keep the stock in his name as collateral for the loan. In such cases, the stock is said to be in "street name," that is, in the name of the Wall Street broker. (See also STREET.)

Strike Price

A term used in buying and selling options to refer to the price stated in the option contract at which the holder of the option can buy or sell the stock. For example, if he buys a call on one hundred shares of General Motors at $55 each, the strike price (that is, the price at which he can buy the General Motors) is $55.

The strike price is also known as the "exercise price."

Summer Soldiers

Officers or directors of a company who put up only a token resistance when faced with an unfriendly takeover. (See also SHARK REPELLENTS, KILLER BEES.)

Summer soldiers

Supply-Side Tax Cuts

Cuts based on an economic theory holding that the best way to increase employment and reduce inflation is to cut taxes. Lower taxes supposedly encourage people and businesses to produce more, because they will keep more of what they earn; these higher production levels will then create more jobs, reducing unemployment. Moreover, because there will be more goods and services available as a result of the higher production levels, there will be less pressure for prices to increase, so the rate of inflation will also decrease.

Support Level

Once a stock sells above the price at which a good deal of buying and selling previously occurred, this old price level is said to represent "support." For example, if Xerox traded between $44 a share and $47 a share for several months, and then moved to 50, the 44–47 price range is the support level. Supposedly, all the people who saw it sell between 44 and 47 and *didn't* buy it then are kicking themselves for missing that opportunity. Therefore, if the stock returns to the 44–47 range, they will buy it, thus "supporting" the price at that level. (See also RESISTANCE LEVEL.)

Swap

A maneuver in which the investor sells one security and replaces it with an equivalent one. One version is "tax swapping." Here, an investor sells a stock or bond in which he has a loss, so that the loss can be deducted when he computes his annual tax bill. At the same time, however, he replaces this stock or bond with a similar one. For example, if he owns one hundred shares of U.S. Steel, which is currently selling at $20 a share, but for which he paid $30, he might sell it, taking a $1,000 loss. Simultaneously, he might buy one hundred shares of Bethlehem Steel, assuming that if U.S. Steel subsequently rises, Bethlehem will, too, since they are both steel companies. In this way, he's had his cake (the tax loss) and eaten it, too, because he continues to retain the potential for appreciation if steel stocks rally.

Tax Evasion, Tax Avoidance

Two methods of cutting one's tax bill. Note, however, that while tax evasion is a crime, tax avoidance (finding as many shelters as possible) is not only legal but also enthusiastically encouraged by lawyers, brokers, and accountants. However, this year's tax-avoidance scheme might turn out, upon examination by the IRS, to have been a form of tax evasion, subjecting one, years later, to unexpected taxes, penalties, and interest payments.

Tax Shelter

Any investment that reduces the tax burden on an individual. Municipal bonds are tax shelters because the interest paid is not subject to federal income taxes; IRA accounts are tax shelters because one doesn't pay current income taxes on the dollars placed in such accounts or on the income these dollars earn. In addition, there are more exotic and riskier tax shelters—cattle raising, airplane leasing, oil drilling, for instance—where many of the costs involved, especially in their earlier years, can be deducted from other income in determining one's overall tax bill.

Tax shelter

T-Bill

A U.S. Treasury bill. This bond is a form of government debt that matures, or comes due, within a year or less of its issue. The Treasury sells three-month and six-month T-bills once a week, usually on a Monday, and sells bills with other maturities periodically throughout the year.

T-bills can be purchased through a bank or broker, or directly from any Federal Reserve bank.

T-Note

A U.S. Treasury note: a debt sold with an original maturity of one to ten years.

Ten-Day Window

Under current laws, if a purchaser buys 5 percent of the stock of a publicly owned company, he must notify the Securities and Exchange Commission within ten days, so that the SEC can let the public know that a possible takeover battle could be brewing. Some experts believe that this ten-day window is open to abuse, because it gives the purchaser a chance to continue buying during the ten days before disclosure is required.

Tender Offer

This is an offer to buy shares of a company that is made to the shareholders by another company or investor group, or in some cases, by the company itself. Often, the price offered is above the current market price, because the purchaser wants to buy a large number of shares—(say, to take control of the company)—and believes that only by offering a very attractive price will he attract sufficient shares.

Thundering Herd

Merrill Lynch Pierce Fenner & Smith, Wall Street's largest brokerage house. The firm has been known by this nickname for many years, well before its advertising campaign which featured herds of cattle stampeding across a TV screen. Another popular nickname for Merrill Lynch is "We The People," presumably developed in response to switchboard operators who, years ago, would answer the phone with the company's full five-partner name.

Tender offer

Thirty-Day Visible Supply

The total dollar amount of municipal-bond issues scheduled for sale during the thirty days following a given date. A very large thirty-day visible supply might suggest that interest rates could rise because of a need to offer higher rates to sell all the new issues. A small thirty-day visible supply might suggest the reverse.

Thirty-day visible supply is reported daily in the Blue List.

Ticker Tape

Years ago, transactions on the New York Stock Exchange and other exchanges were reported via telegraph on paper tape, which flowed from a ticker machine. Thus, "ticker tape" or "reading the tape" became a convenient way of referring simply to activity on the floor of the exchanges. Today, in most cases, transactions are reported on electronic boards with moving lights or on small TV-like screens, but the term *ticker tape* as a way of referring to prices on a stock exchange still persists; one might, for example, phone one's broker and ask him what was doing on the tape.

TIGRs, CATS, and LIONs.

A form of investment, first introduced in 1982, representing ownership of U.S. Treasury bonds along with the interest payments due on them in future years. They are sold at a discount from their eventual cash-in value, pay no income at all during the period of time held, and then pay full cash-in value when due. For example, in mid-1983, $1,000 face-value CATS due in 1988 were selling at around $600. A purchaser would receive no income during the next five years, but in 1988 he would redeem his CATS for $1,000.

These new securities were greeted with enormous enthusiasm by investors when first offered, and several brokerage houses came out with their own versions, all of which are basically similar. TIGRs (Treasury Investment Growth Receipts) were Merrill Lynch's product. CATS (Certificates of Accrual on Treasury Securities) were offered by Prudential-Bache and Salomon, and LIONs (Lehman Investment Opportunity Notes) by Lehman Brothers. Banks and brokers can buy these securities for you. (See also ZERO COUPON BONDS.)

Tombstone ad

Tombstone Ad

Announcement placed in a newspaper or financial magazine reporting a new issue of securities. They are called tombstone ads, according to *Webster's Dictionary,* because of their "staid, unexciting character." This remark is, if anything, an understatement, since the advertisements include not much more than the name of the new issue and a lengthy listing of the financial firms handling the deal.

Ton

Bond traders' jargon for $100 million.

Totten Trust

A misnomer, since a Totten Trust isn't really a trust at all. It's actually a bank account an individual may open in his name "in trust for" someone else. During his lifetime, he may add or withdraw funds at any time, and the person named "in trust" has no rights at all in connection with the account. At the holder's death, however, the money is payable directly to the beneficiary, usually without probate, although it does not escape estate taxes if they would otherwise be due.

A Totten trust is one way of arranging for someone to inherit a specific part of property (the bank account) without mentioning it in one's will.

Trashing the Market

Issuing so much of a particular kind of security so as to cause its prices to fall.

Two-Dollar Broker

A member of the New York Stock Exchange who executes order for other members. For example, if an investor enters an order at his local office of Dean Witter to buy one hundred shares of Commonwealth Edison (a stock traded on the New York Stock Exchange), Dean Witter's order room phones it down to their floor broker, a representative of the firm who is a member of the New York Stock Exchange and who normally handles buy and sell orders entered there by Dean Witter's customers. However, if, this broker is too busy to handle the order, Dean Witter's clerk will give it to another floor broker to handle, paying him a small part of the commission the investor will pay on the trade. Years ago, the standard fee paid to such brokers was $2; today it varies, but use of *two-dollar* broker persists.

Underwriter

A financial organization that handles sales of new securities which a corporation or municipality wishes to sell in order to raise money. Typically, the underwriters will buy the securities—say, a new issue of bonds—from the company at a stated price, and then resell them at once to the public at a slightly higher price. Underwriters also sometimes perform similar services for individuals who own large blocks of stock—for example, when disposing of holdings for the founding family of a company. In most cases, by law, underwriters are investment-banking or brokerage firms; however, commercial banks are also permitted to underwrite certain kinds of issues, such as municipal bonds.

Universal Life

A form of life insurance introduced in 1978 by E. F. Hutton Life Insurance Co. (an affiliate of the brokerage house) and now offered by many companies. It is an insurance package consisting of life insurance plus an investment in a money fund. The client pays one premium, but he may choose to use part of it to buy term insurance, and the rest to invest in a money fund. Periodically, as his needs change, he may change his allocation to buy more insurance and put less in the money fund, or vice versa.

Uptick, Downtick

An uptick is a transaction made at a price higher than the previous one. For example, if one hundred shares of U.S. Steel trade at 20⅛ and then another one hundred at 20¼, the latter trade is an uptick. Downticks are trades made at a price lower than the previous transaction.

Universal life

Vestal Virgin

A term used to identify a group of stocks favored by institutional investment managers during the late 1960s and early 1970s. These stocks, like the temple virgins of Ancient Rome, had spotless reputations and were considered impeccable investment choices. Unfortunately, they also had very high price/earnings ratios and, periodically since 1974, earnings difficulties, with the result that during the late 1970s many dropped precipitously from their former highs (although some have recovered since then and have gone on to sell at even higher prices). Vestal Virgins included IBM, Avon, Polaroid, Simplicity, MMM, International Flavors and Fragrances, and Tampax. They were also known as the "nifty fifty."

Vestal virgin

White Knight

If a company is threatened by a takeover from outsiders who are considered unfriendly (for example, outsiders who might fire all of the current management) and it feels it cannot fight off the attacker on its own, it may look for a friendly savior. The idea is that if one must be taken over, it's better to have an amicable acquirer—that is, a "white knight," rather than a hostile black knight. With this in mind, a broker might tell his client not to sell XYZ stock at $48 a share in the face of an offer from the Jones Co., because he believes that XYZ is desperately looking for a white knight who might offer more.

Whoops!

The nickname for Washington Public Power Supply System (WPPSS), a consortium of utilities companies that banded together during the 1970s to build nuclear electric plants in the Pacific Northwest. Originally, the nickname was used merely as a convenient shorthand way of pronouncing the otherwise unpronounceable WPPSS. However, as financial problems and default confronted the consortium, and the consortium subsequently defaulted in 1983, the term was employed more frequently, often followed by an exclamation point, as an indication of the unexpected difficulties facing the system.

White knight

Whoops!

Window Dressing

A maneuver often engaged in by mutual funds at the end of the quarter (around the 25th of March, June, September, and December) in order to impress stockholders who will be receiving a report showing the fund's holdings. One way to impress them is to make it seem as if the fund has been clever enough to own those stocks which have been particularly profitable during the quarter; thus, if IBM, Texaco, and Phelps Dodge have all been up sharply during the preceding three months, a fund might buy these stocks on March 28 so that it could show them as part of its March 31 portfolio.

Window dressing

X Dividend

A term meaning "without dividend." A stock bought on or after the X-dividend day will not pay the purchaser the next dividend. For example, if General Motors goes X-dividend on March 15, with the next dividend payable on April 10, an investor would get that dividend if he bought the stock on March 14, which is *before* the X-dividend date, but not if he bought it on or after March 15.

All other things being equal, the market price of the stock normally drops by the amount of the dividend on the day it goes X-dividend.

Yankee Bank, Yankee CDs

A Yankee bank is a branch of a foreign bank operating in the U.S. For example, the New York branch of the Bank of Tokyo would be a Yankee bank, and the Certificates of Deposit that it issues would be called Yankee CDs.

Yard

Foreign-exchange traders' nickname for one billion Japanese yen.

Yankee bank

Yield to maturity

Year-End Migration

A term referring to the Defense Department's practice of "reprogramming" unspent money left from one project at the end of the year to another project. The expression might, for instance, be used by a broker to explain why a Defense Department supplier's prospects looked bright: "Year-end migration monies should provide Co. X with unexpected sales for the upcoming year."

Yield to Maturity

The rate of return an investor is actually earning on a bond taking into account not only the stated interest rate, but also the price paid for it and the maturity date. For example, if an investor bought a 6 percent $1,000 face-value bond due in ten years for $800, it would pay him $60 a year currently on his $800 investment, or $7\frac{1}{2}$ percent. (See also CURRENT YIELD.) However, in ten years, he would get back $1,000, or $200 more than he had invested. The yield to maturity takes into consideration that additional $200, and would therefore show that he was actually earning about 9 percent over the 10-year period, rather than the apparent $7\frac{1}{2}$ percent.

Bonds selling for less than $1,000 will have a yield to maturity higher than the stated interest rate, as the above example illustrates; bonds selling for more than $1,000 will have a yield to maturity that is lower than the stated yield. When professionals quote bond yields, they are almost always referring to yield to maturity.

Your Federal Income Tax

Also known as Publication 17, this is a free, excellent guide (two hundred pages plus) to preparing your personal federal income-tax return issued by the IRS. It is revised annually and is available upon request from any local IRS office.

Zero Coupon Bond

A bond that pays no interest while the investor holds it. It is sold originally at a substantial discount from its eventual maturity value, paying the investor its full face value when it comes due, with the difference between what he paid initially and what he finally collected representing the interest he *would* have received over the years it was held. (See also TIGRs, CATS, and LIONs.)